P9-CEN-634

SOUNDS LIKE READING™

BOOK TWO

Stop, Drop, and Flop in the Slop

A SHORT VOWEL SOUNDS BOOK WITH CONSONANT BLENDS

Brian P. Cleary

illustrations by

Jason Miskimins

Consultant:
Alice M. Maday
Ph.D. in Early Childhood Education with a Focus in Literacy
Assistant Professor, Retired
Department of Curriculum and Instruction
University of Minnesota

M Millbrook Press/Minneapolis

to Sister Mary Jude,
my first-grade teacher in Mission, Kansas
—B.P.C.

Text copyright © 2009 by Brian P. Cleary
Illustrations copyright © 2009 by Lerner Publishing Group, Inc.

All rights reserved. International copyright secured. No part of this book may
be reproduced, stored in a retrieval system, or transmitted in any form or by any
means—electronic, mechanical, photocopying, recording, or otherwise—without
the prior written permission of Lerner Publishing Group, Inc., except for the
inclusion of brief quotations in an acknowledged review.

Millbrook Press
A division of Lerner Publishing Group, Inc.
241 First Avenue North
Minneapolis, MN 55401 U.S.A.

Website address: www.lernerbooks.com

Library of Congress Cataloging-in-Publication Data

Cleary, Brian P., 1959–
    Stop, drop, and flop in the slop : a short vowel sounds book with consonant
blends / by Brian P. Cleary ; illustrations by Jason Miskimins ; consultant:
Alice M. Maday.
        p.   cm. — (Sounds like reading)
    ISBN 978-0-8225-7635-8 (lib. bdg. : alk. paper)
    1. English language—Vowels—Juvenile literature. 2. English language—
Consonants—Juvenile literature. 3. English language—Phonetics—Juvenile
literature. 4. Reading—Phonetic method—Juvenile literature. I. Miskimins,
Jason, ill. II. Maday, Alice M. III. Title.
PE1157.C56 2009
428.1'3—dc22   2008012777

Manufactured in the United States of America
1 2 3 4 5 6 – BP – 14 13 12 11 10 09

Dear Parents and Educators,

As a former adult literacy coach and the father of three children, I know that learning to read isn't always easy. That's why I developed **Sounds Like Reading**™—a series that uses a combination of devices to help children learn to read.

This book is the second in the **Sounds Like Reading**™ series. It uses rhyme, repetition, illustration, and phonics to introduce young readers to short vowel sounds and consonant blends— "sound-outable" letter combinations such as *cl, tr, br,* and *st.*

Starting on page 4, you'll see three rhyming words on each left-hand page. These words are part of the sentence on the facing page. They all feature short vowels and consonant blends. As the book progresses, the sentences become more challenging. These sentences contain a "discovery" word—an extra rhyming word in addition to those that appear on the left. Toward the end of the book, the sentences contain two discovery words. Children will delight in the increased confidence that finding and decoding these words will bring. They'll also enjoy looking for the mouse that appears throughout the book. The mouse asks readers to look for words that sound alike.

The bridge to literacy is one of the most important we will ever cross. It is my hope that the **Sounds Like Reading**™ series will help young readers to hop, gallop, and skip from one side to the other!

Sincerely,

Brian P. Cleary

Look for me to help you find the words that sound alike!

clam

swam

tram

The **clam swam** in the **tram**.

plum

drum

glum

Can you find three words that sound alike?

The **plum** on the **drum** is **glum**.

drink

stink

blink

Can you find the word that sounds like drink, stink, and blink?

The **drink** from the **rink** had
such a **stink**, it made him **blink**.

Fred

sped

sled

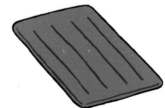

Can you find the word that sounds like Fred, sped, and sled?

Fred sped his **sled** by the **bed**.

stop

drop

slop

Can you find the word that sounds like stop, drop, and slop?

Stop, **drop**, and **flop** in the **slop**.

glass

brass

grass

Can you find the word that sounds like glass, brass, and grass?

14

The **glass** and the **brass** were on the **grass** after **class**.

frog

clog

smog

Can you find the word that sounds like frog, clog, and smog?

16

The **frog** by the **clog** is in a **fog** of **smog**.

stump

plump

grump

Can you find the word that sounds like stump, plump, and grump?

18

The **stump** and the **lump** are by
the **plump grump**.

drab

crab

grab

Can you find the word that sounds like drab, crab, and grab?

20

The **drab crab** can **grab** his **scab**.

grid

slid

skid

Can you find the word that sounds like grid, slid, and skid?

22

The **grid slid** and made the **kid skid.**

Scott

trot

Spot

Can you find two words that sound like Scott, trot, and Spot?

24

Scott got to **trot** with **Spot** to the **plot**.

spell

swell

smell

Can you find two words that sound like spell, swell, and smell?

Nell can **spell** *swell* by the **well**
with the **smell**.

slug

snug

plug

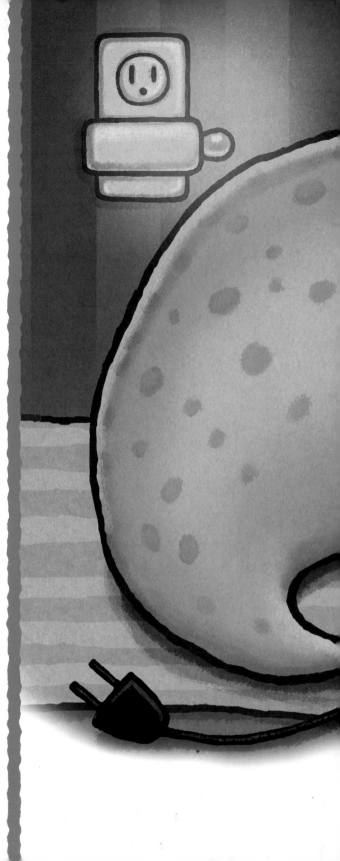

Can you find two words that sound like slug, snug, and plug?

The **slug** and **pug** slept **snug** on the **rug** by the **plug**.

slim

skim

brim

Can you find two words that sound like slim, skim, and brim?

Slim Kim drank a cup of **skim**
filled to the **brim** after a **swim**.

Brian P. Cleary is the author of the best-selling Words Are CATegorical® series as well as the Math Is CATegorical® and Adventures in Memory™ series. He has also written several picture books and poetry books. In addition to his work as a children's author and humorist, Mr. Cleary has been a tutor in an adult literacy program. He lives in Cleveland, Ohio.

Jason Miskimins grew up in Cincinnati, Ohio, and graduated from the Columbus College of Art & Design in 2003. He currently lives in North Olmsted, Ohio, where he works as an illustrator of books and greeting cards.

Alice M. Maday has a master's degree in early childhood education from Butler University in Indianapolis, Indiana, and a Ph.D. in early childhood education, with a focus in literacy, from the University of Minnesota in Minneapolis. Dr. Maday has taught at the college level as well as in elementary schools and preschools throughout the country. In addition, she has served as an emergent literacy educator for kindergarten and first-grade students in Germany for the U.S. Department of Defense. Her research interests include the kindergarten curriculum, emergent literacy, parent and teacher expectations, and the place of preschool in the reading readiness process.

For even more phonics fun, check out all eight SOUNDS LIKE READING™ titles listed on the back of this book!

And find activities, games, and more at www.brianpcleary.com.

Pb **CLEAR**
Cleary, Brian P., 1959-
Stop, drop, and flop in the slop
: a short vowel sounds book
with consonant blends /

0006102524573

outr

Dayton Metro Library

Easy

No longer property of the
Dayton Metro Library